AUSCULTATE

Copyright © 2025 Clayton Adam Clark
ISBN 978-0-913123-47-8

First published by Galileo Books
FREEGALILEO.COM

Book design by Adam Robinson
Author Photo by Tina Marelina Clark
Edited by Barrett Warner

AUSCULTATE

Poems
by
Clayton Adam Clark

CONTENTS

First Chamber — 1

Self-portrait With Leap-second Vigil — 3
The Auto Plant — 5
Buzzing Beneath the Leaves — 6
Firebreak — 8
Leeches — 10
Gooseflesh — 11
Tornado Season — 12
Paresthesia — 13

Second Chamber — 15

Autumn Congregations — 17
Bald — 18
Fistulas — 19
Auscultation — 21
Reverberations — 22
Brood — 24
Sleepwalk Mannerism — 25
Skinned — 26
Coalescence — 28

Third Chamber 31

The Tornado Siren 33
Caprinae 34
Mutton 35
Mousing 36
Figure II 38
Fungicide Blues 39
Flight Theory 40
Backbones 41
Prayer to the Transporter 43
The Missouri 44

Fourth Chamber 47

Only Not Like This))) 49
Consumed 50
Nautili 52
House Centipede 53
1983 54
Corn 55
The Hoarder's Epilogue 56
Ribcage 57
Preserve 58
Attrition 59

Fifth Chamber 61

ACKNOWLEDGEMENTS

Thank you to the Galileo Press team for the honor of bringing this book into the world, especially Barrett Warner, whose enthusiasm, imagination, & sound editorial feedback pushed my poems forward into the work I'm proud you get to read today. I'm truly appreciative of this opportunity to collaborate.

I remain grateful to & fond of my mentors @ Ohio State, especially poets Andrew Hudgins, Henri Cole, & Kathy Fagan, who'd help guide many of these poems early on, as well as Michelle Herman, Lee Martin, Erin McGraw, & the late Lee K. Abbott. Same goes for Bill Riley, Gabriel Urza, Derek Palacio, Alex "the Great" Streiff, Daniel Carter, Matthew Sumpter, & my other classmates, including my poet cohort: Jones Ellenberger, Lo Kwa Mei-en, Benjamin Gloss, Allison Pitinii Davis, & Tory Adkisson. So many fond memories, you guys.

Friends, family, parents, grandparents, & brothers — you know who you are. I thank you for all you've done that shaped me toward this particular here & now. I treasure the opportunity to share these words with you.

And finally, I'm a lifetime of thankful to my wife, Tina, who chose me & has continued to choose me every day since. That means more to me than I will ever fully be able to express. But trust me, I will keep trying to. Most of all, I love you & our furry family & this life we're choosing together. ♡

Lots of love,
CAC

I'm also grateful to the editors @ magazines who took a chance on giving some of these poems their first lives on a printed page or screen:

32 Poems: "Caprinae"

Asheville Poetry Review: "Coalescence"

Birmingham Poetry Review: "The Tornado Siren"

Blue Earth Review: "Tornado Season" and "House Centipede"

Chariton Review: "Self-portrait With Leap-second Vigil"

Cold Mountain Review: "Attrition"

Cottonwood: "Backbones"

Fearsome Critters Arts Journal: "Firebreak" and "The Missouri"

Fourteen: "Autumn Congregations"

Glassworks Magazine: "Sleepwalk Mannerism" and "Skinned"

The Greensboro Review: "Nautili"

The Kentucky Review: "Mousing" and "1983"

Los Angeles Review: "Fistulas"

The Louisiana Review: "Mutton"

The McNeese Review: "The Auto Plant," "Auscultation" (as "Public Imagination"), "Brood," "Prayer to the Transporter," and "Consumed"

Natural Bridge: "Paresthesia"

New Plains Review: "Buzzing Beneath the Leaves"

Ocean State Review: "Ribcage"

Permafrost: "Bald" (as "Her Arrangements Will Be Nice")

Portland Review: "Leeches" and "Corn"

Sierra Nevada Review: "Reverberations" and "The Hoarder's Epilogue"

Slipstream: "Flight Theory"

William & Mary Review: "Fungicide Blues"

First Chamber

Self-portrait With Leap-second Vigil

Snow halts, so I can see beyond
the weather outside: across the street
    my building is reflected
        in the gold-sheened windows

of another building. Six months ago a second
was added to this day, and I just found
my window in the reflections. Whoever
first observed summer turn autumn

then winter must have felt abandoned in those,
the longest months ever. Now we know to add
a second once or twice a year to keep our time
    aligned with Earth's rotation,

        what with it dragging
water against space and not keeping up
with the frantic oscillations of caesium-133.
No way that first witness devised guilt:

what fear to watch the ground die beneath
your feet. Who could shoulder such blame,
    the out-and-out demise?
        With Earth never turning

faster than time, it must be monitored:
an earthquake in the ocean knocks us
out of sync. I didn't feel it cracking
across the globe, all 2.68 microseconds

Earth stood still, but others learned the weight
of leveled buildings, and here I am straining
to see my silhouette across a span of street.
Each body is a building, and my wristwatch

keeps ticking, too, but it suffers
    clock drift like everything else.
        Earth may have created
the sins, but man called them, fixing them

outside our buildings to point and gape at.
How many more we can find in reflection.
    I peer through a one-way mirror
        to see my own golden eyes,

like I could conquer the space between
my selves. No, it's a single body marked
on granite with two dates: this one moved
this many winters. If we're not vigilant,

noon slides into midnight or vice versa
    and the dates lose meaning
        because the ocean doesn't quit
grasping for all it doesn't hold, and astigmatic,

I will not see myself. It didn't exist,
    a single first person
        who beheld winter alone,
but it's easier to understand a lone man,

balled up beneath leaves in a gulley
uphill of his river, who learns the need
to build while crying out against the fire
    burning beneath his fingers' blistered skin.

The Auto Plant

Three thousand feet of interstate frontage
and a *For Sale* sign big as a trailer, here
is where we can't grow. The fathers and mothers
retired early with pensions, one taking leave

of house payments and setting aside the closing
costs for his grown daughters: two weddings. They'll reap
copious gifts. Once poured as a factory floor,
powdered-stone-and-water's struck and strewn

as fresh rocks—a soiled skin of broken parts—
and presumed fallow. But oil, like loss, soaks down
who-knows-how-far. Two hundred ninety-five
acres of floodplain seized from The Meramec

               just upriver of the landfill where
methane greens a twilight bank reception.

Buzzing Beneath the Leaves

> —*Centennial Park, Nashville, Tennessee*

Music gambols off a stage
between two oaks greater around
than any bass drum or the country-

gospel-jazz-blues that unloads
from bruised amps. *We're lucky to have
this weather*, the emcee reminds us

between sets. The park is something left
alone and not, trees thriving like rests
before strummed chords. A tree I don't

recognize flutters with heart-shaped
leaves not shaped like actual hearts,
but the lean of its trunk reminds me

of my backbone, its compression.
The shirtless man our emcee identified
as Ricky dances all songs at the stage's foot,

fingers exploding for crash cymbals,
back pumped from hunch to upright,
clavicle-wrenching chorus, and his long hair

covers his spine when he stills between
the songs. The frequencies must survive
inside there, trapped and shaking the bones

that rivet him at rest. After a while, children
gravitate to Ricky, but one boy dances
facing us: backflips, high kicks. He's good,

but his moves aren't driven by the drums.
He grooves alone in the mass like the two
giant oaks, their roots seizing the earth

to hold plumb. The music doesn't guide
this boy the way it does the pit-shaped
crowd, all buzzing beneath the leaves

in time, but there's nobody who doesn't
feel the earth's reining us in, rain
the prodding reminder that we share

one course of movement. After the show,
I watch a fountain in the man-made pond
keep algae lapping at a stone wall

instead of overcrowding the water,
this movement preserving a surface
where the earth reflects the sky.

Firebreak

—After West Lake Landfill, Bridgeton, Missouri

A rat scuttled ahead of me, trailing
the corner where the sidewalk met

cinderblock wall, until it found ingress
to one of the last abandoned buildings

in my neighborhood. Delivery trucks coaled
each house, offloading fuel in yards,

when my grandfather grew up here,
and mothers paid boys movie fare

to shuttle it down chutes. Dodging rats
between brick homes until they emptied

their shovels, the boys culled slow rats,
a *twang* of shovelhead resounding

up and out the narrow, shaded space.
Today, my city's lights are coal-fired,

and the retired north landfill has burned
flameless in its bowels for the past

ten years. I didn't know oxygen bled
so far subsurface. The Army Corps

of Engineers had to bury a firebreak
as the burn wormed closer to some legacy

nuclear waste interred in World War II.
There's talk of rats, when this ends,

assuming the role of dominant species.
Maybe they learn how, in time, to burn

our epoch or build with it. Calcareous
fossils and carbonate mud lithified

beneath the weight of shallow seas,
limestone remains here. My coal chute

is bricked up and the furnace burns clear
natural gas, but the limestone steps

to my front door still green with lichen.
Like my grandfather before me, I've scrubbed

dirt and base plant life from the porous slabs.
It was from that rock I saw a night crawler

wriggling into the street below. I foresaw
the desert life before it, have seen the dead

worm on pavement animated by a legion
of ants. With a stick I tried to save the annelid,

tossing it in my yard for our mutual benefit
of its devotion to the soil, only to see it writhe

its way back to the concrete, fleeing clover
I'd sprayed with chemicals the day before,

earth burning with the fire you only feel.

Leeches

After hunting mussels from shoreline rocks,
          my brothers and I pinched leeches
     from our legs while our catch boiled
on the fire. The three-toothed parasites
          tugged at our skin, released, and then writhed
     on the embers where we flicked them.
One clamped onto my thumb before
          it went, a clawing I admire and evidence
     for what I fear to find beneath the surface.
Even sautéed and salted, the mussels
          weren't good, but we'd taken them so we ate
     all we could and fed all we couldn't
          back to the dark, green water.

Gooseflesh

—After the Creepy Crawl, St. Louis, Missouri

Body heat leaches into winter thickened

between us. On Tucker Ave. post-show, clouds rise

from heads and the gooseflesh beneath our sweat-

through shirts. Young, I feel my fleeing always

as give-and-take—for scapulae to touch,

my sternal skin has to stretch drum-tight. Pulling

coats on, we shiver in the hatchback, dying

to migrate from here, but we must hold for breath

that crystallized on the windshield to soften.

Tornado Season

Butterflies mated in the mimosa tree behind my father's house.
We pulled weeds and then hoisted stones up from the woods

to contain a flowerbed. My father shocked the fountain
with chlorine while I sprayed neurotoxins on a wasp nest

beneath the deck. We did what you do to keep the unwanted
species out, and as it was spring, our bodies did the same.

Scleral capillaries full, we sneezed and blew mucus out,
rejecting the trees' advances. I wasn't always this way.

Once, I sniped a robin with a BB gun and, seeing the body
plummet in the woods, I sprinted toward it with a flooding hope

the bird was only stunned. I've tried to be more preemptive since.
I swallow antihistamines when oak pollen yellows the world,

and I store blankets, food, and water in the basement. Behind
my home, a pair of robins has nested in the carport's tresses.

Due to bird shit parading across my car, then a broken egg,
I considered relocation, but it was too late—the hatchlings

peeked their eyes and gaping beaks above the crest.
I can't shake my feeling that displacement is a human

instinct, but I let them alone. They fledged, surrendering
my home a few weeks later, so I stretched a plastic net

beneath the rafters and hung mirrors—mirrors portray
my place as inhabited so the birds displace themselves—

the mirrors that made me see myself above myself.

Paresthesia

At midday, when the sunlight's angle
of incidence is greatest, the fly trapped
between storm window and window

bides time like a child left in the car
while his parent buys groceries
or the videogames my brother played

so much they stuck in his brain. One night
he ripped books from the shelf in search
of *The Legend of Zelda*'s triforce

while asleep. If words are purified
by scream, an eight-year-old's slurred,
repeated, *I need the triforce* is obsession

embodied when it shakes a family
awake. My mother wrestled him
from the highest shelves, some castle

gate, and held him to the carpet
until he blinked his way back to us.
Paresthesia means the tingling out:

my brother thrashes atop a pile of Little
Golden Books, the fly discovers a crack
in the corner where the window frame

fails square. Phantom needles in the foot
after pressure on the peripheral nerve
withdraws aren't as scary as knowledge

that damage has already begun. Once,
Mom in a store, I touched her car's cigarette
lighter to see if it would really hurt. Dumbly

nursing my thumb in a cup of milk,
I squinted through the early blistering
while my brother distracted her

on the way home. He's a doctor now.
Given the festering wounds and viscera
he's seen, I worry about what sticks.

Deep in a twenty-four-hour shift, he steals
some rest in the rack room—would he
purify all his Latin words or rise

as the flesh of our cavernous insides? He might
finally find the true names for laceration,
deep-vein thrombosis, thermodynamics

of the brain. How fast dream-sense gets lost,
the mind enthralls with reason once the body
begins to move. But not for him. He'd wake,

six stitches in to closing a woman's foot
and telling her things about the untold spots
on her lung he envisioned, then blink, blink blink.

Second Chamber

Autumn Congregations

The leaves gather around an oak tree's base
and the grave markers.

> *I never knew*
> *it was hot*

Algae, sticks, and Styrofoam clumps dam
beneath the bridge to home.

> *in the center*
> *I touched it once*

All the cold pools
at the bottom
of the hill, but we
get warm
walking up.

> *then I touched it again*

Bald

A weight of fluid and excess cells—first, curable,
then not—sat down heaviest in the gut
of a mother. She called her sons' friends sons
more than once, and her eldest called his friends
on the telephone to give the givens of all
of his and their prognosticated loss.

I've heard you don't shave your head
in solidarity, but they hadn't. She wielded
shears on their deck that overlooks the drainage
pond and laughed and laughed as the nest
of hair from her husband's and her boys'
and her boys' friends' heads covered her toes.

Little medicine left and hard-earned needs
to mend, we do and do long as we can,
long as we can not attend to our own bodies,
like gourmet desserts I sent instead of flowers
to this woman—with her two-week body
eviction notice—even though I know her sons

and husband will gorge themselves on the platters
of funerary leftovers. It's so fucking barren here
in February, and she likes chocolate-covered fruit.

Fistulas

Once everyone left your mother's wake, we trudged
down to the drainage pond where we played hockey
in sturdier winters, and one tragic August,

its fountain broke and stilled water grew thick
with pond scum and mosquito hordes too fierce
for citronella. We drank and smoked, the bank

soaked through with melted snow, and didn't talk
about her until I grew so full a cry
squeezed through the fistula my throat had become.

Because you had two months to mourn with her,
you reached your hand for my back faster than I
expected when I sobbed and retched in the pond.

I slept on the basement couch, your dad asleep
in their bed two stories up, and woke at dawn
with muddy shoes by the sliding glass door.

The bagpipes played that day, their drone two octaves
below the tonic, and in my black suit,
I passed out tissues to the bereaved, the box

of cardboard hollowing in my hands. I drove
home after, and the trap in my cupboard
she first taught me to make with a soda bottle

swarmed with fruit flies. They entered a hole on top
to feast what was left of their two-week lives
on chunks of browning banana, not to find

again how they'd come in. They don't stop breeding,
five hundred eggs per female, so I took
the bottle out with the trash. I don't lament this.

You mailed me her picture, and I spent the week
clapping my hands on flies that never found
the trap or even knew a trap existed.

Auscultation

The man goes at and at and at the woman, hard enough
that keepsakes tremble from the dresser, till he finishes.

He exits, showers—she contorts to clean him off her back.
Sometimes I'd think this exciting. Other times I'd want

to punish him for not holding her after. She wipes herself
and him off with the sheets—still crisp, unwashed—he bought last month

after his wife died. Maybe he flipped the mattress and hollowed
their room of her effects, but he must have lain there—dormant—

for the three years her cervix annulled her body inside out.
Sometimes a body's currency, abrading as unseen parts

are lost to hands that possess it. Of course, the neighbors notice
the car parked at his house each night. *Didn't he love his wife?*

they think, then say. A penny placed on railroad tracks is worth
nothing except some copper fused with zinc after the train.

If I wake up to the storm windows rattling, I know
it isn't wind I hear but plastic shuddering in its tracks.

Grasping with whatever's at hand—the doctor who auscultated
the widower's wife, placing the stethoscope here, here, and there

till they knew something—have we hoped to get it with our prying?
The woman never parks in the driveway. She walks the lawn—

sometimes he cracks the door before she can knock. Surely they feel
the air that must be exhaled when he lets her body in.

Reverberations

When the front wall of my home shook
and moaned last summer, I ran out the back door

to stand in the yard, not the duck and cover
I trained for in school. My neighbor's shepherd

barked the whole time I waited for the toppling.
Another time, the windows crooned as a plane,

low-flying, passed with two pitches: the steepness
of its westerly ascent and that of my windows.

Hundreds of people thousands of feet above
vibrated at a rate my windows sang to.

I felt no other indication of their leaving.
My neighbor's dog barks at everyone it sees.

Inside my house I hear it bark at the mailperson
from inside my neighbor's house—sound goes

out and in then in to me. This is the nature
of feedback. Debarking surgery is an option,

though cruel for a dog that so much loves
its instrument. One fall, I watched a red-tailed

hawk fly over desiccated corn stalks, tipping
its pitch to pull a circle and cross the parallels

of furrowed earth. It dove but pulled up
at the stalk line. If the rodent had run

the ditch much longer, I could've seen it borne
in talons to the nearest grove. The hawk

tears its prey open, causing the cries to stop,
but I can't imagine that noise—its perpetuation

or cessation—has any faltering effect
on the hawk. Envious of instincts, I

keep trying to learn. Another instinct?
My neighbor installed a wooden fence

so when I grill out back, the dog barks,
I hear you, I hear you, I can hear you instead

of *I see you, I see you*, and sometimes
my neighbor yells, *Shut up*. The dog is true

to its need to bark, and its vocal cords
slap together at a rate that hurts inside

my ear canals, so I'm learning it's me
that must change. Some proof I might: a giant,

winged shadow and roaring clamor pass above me
on my walk to work. I neither run nor hide.

Brood

    Because the children walked the dogs that summer
        on leashes with choke chains—the metal-pronged,
            not slipknot steel, just sharp enough to pinch

    enough to yoke—and because the parents split
        and worked to pay their lawyers, the children grew
            accustomed to wielding cheap tennis racquets

    in humid hands not yanked by mutts and swatting
        cicadas that dive-bombed from trees. The heads
            stuck in the squares and had to be poked out

    with sticks while on the sidewalk bodies whirled
        and the dogs sniffed then sometimes chewed the sour,
            crunchy abdomens but seldom swallowed.

    Because that year both thirteen- and seventeen-
        year broods erupted from the earth together,
            the eldest boy found a swarm filling the hollow

    base of an elm, and after he loosed the dog
        to the backyard's chain-link confines, he grabbed
            WD-40 from the cardboard box

    bearing his father's name in his mom's garage.
        The neighbor boys, his brothers, watched him spray
            the throng. They counted down, each with his own

    lighter ready, and cheered for the squirming
        panic they could set fire because because.

Sleepwalk Mannerism

A long neck and some mustard light
in the flat glass, the mirror, your eyes
shutter. A goose—there was a goose.

Sit on the toilet and pee. Remember
its fur, not feathers. *Buy me a burger*,
it said, squatting on stairs, its neck

writhing herky jerky. Your neck
was elongated just now, slender
at best. You didn't buy the goose

a burger. Its timbre matched the man's
on High by Wendy's—*Spare some change*.
You bolted. Sensible, given the squawking

goose, lurid like the jangling cup—
Dixie—you pass each way to work.
Flush. You're less Parmagianinian

in the mirror now, less serpentine
and more natural, albeit less
of you, but the heart—*where's your heart, friend?*—

still pounds, and though you didn't pee
in the trashcan again, the excess
cervical vertebrae weren't yours

to keep. The *Where are you?* from bed.
You can't go back. Beyond the light
your skin's a scarf tasseled with thumping

carotids. You must miss the ornate
brass doorknob, reaching a hand no longer
artful, the fingers now to scale.

Skinned

After three days no-call, no-show at work,
police found him hanging by the heirloom belt.
His parents called her, a thousand miles away

—one of the first. *Fly in for the services?*
Of course. *Eat dinner with them?* Of course.
It's been too long. After a shower, she rubbed

a towel down her arms until she recognized
their hair. She always thought it grew
in the same grain as the muscles beneath,

but it didn't. Sweat welled up in her pores,
triggered by steam that settled much
like dust in the kitchen of his family's cottage.

She sat on the tub ledge and, with a cheap razor,
shaved each forearm and the muted fuzz
above her humerus. She couldn't find his note

in the red nicks around her elbow
but wondered if she gouged her finger
into a cut, would she, boring past capillaries

to veins that rushed her back to her heart
that shoved her forth to the cliff ledges
of her body, would she ever arrive

where their cells commingled still,
a cottage bedroom, the quilt they'd loved on,
their fluids dried as one stain, or any edge

she could reach inside his body from—
could she thrust her fingers through
the cave-in he forged from his trachea,

birthing a welcome aperture to draw red
into his lungs then heart then arteries, down
to waken feet that scrabble the closet floor

for stance, the tingles of sleep's needles
pricking his soles as the skin of a cow,
now dead for generations, bears his weight

to rise. Her bones were her bones. She could
bury herself in layers of him like the honest
weight of the quilt that burdened her body

to the bed that winter. She was touching
her humerus, one of its knobby ends,
and felt the tendons clutching true.

Coalescence

The neighbor hovered over
a broken trail of zoysia
(tall beer in hand) until

it moved, then plunged a pitchfork
into the mole below.
My stepfather trapped

raccoons (that may have bitten
his dog) in a steel cage
and heaved them, cage and all,

into a lake, then waited
for the water to still.
Once, my mother kept

alive a rabbit I'd clipped
with the mower (*gorked*, she called it)
three days on analeptics,

feeding it like a baby.
(But I can't recall if
we buried it.) Today,

my grandmother lives on
machines and under ice
packs that keep her brain

small enough to fit
inside her skull, and even
my mother has said, *The questions*

of quality of life
may need to be asked. Deaths
coalesce with deaths

like the ice cube that melts
in my rocks glass, and I
barely sense them. (Our dog

still pees beneath the tree
where we buried its mother.)
I drive to join my family

to turn off the machines
and either greet my wakened
grandma or watch the water

until it stills. No deaths
can prepare us. A hawk
snatching off a piece

of road-kill armadillo
takes flight from the highway
to flee my dark sedan.

Third Chamber

The Tornado Siren

It blares and hums and blares, two dogs sing,
and birds crowd on a branch. From my deck I watch
a plastic bag, snagged on the limb last month,
convulsing in the wind, and when it slackens
I smell the cardboard box, weighted with sand,
I glutted with last winter's cigarettes.

I could think of Yeats or Milton, search
the sky for gyres and Jesus, but it's Monday,
the first this month. It's hard to know if seething,
green clouds deserve my panic or if it's all
a drill. If I heave the box into the dumpster,
will I suddenly be prepared for spring?

I let the tattered plastic fly through summer,
a winter's flag, as children battle choices
beside the ice cream truck. One child might trickle
a handful of coins, and maybe the last dime
clings to her palm before she makes it go.
I want to tell this girl in blue galoshes

to save her mother's change. The rains do come,
slowly at first but then enough to scatter
to porches the children hunching over treats.
The ice cream man bleats his ragtime and trolls
the street for one last patron, a kind of hope
that I admire in all the after-silence.

Caprinae

It was a Sunday after church, his mother
driving the van she won in the divorce.
She quizzed him on the sermon, *to reinforce
your learning*, while in back his younger brother
watched his cartoons. He told her he liked the choice
in Matthew to be a goat or sheep, that we
could do good deeds and be safe. *Someday we'll see
your rutting father burn*, she said, *and rejoice*.

When he confessed at last to moving in
with his girlfriend, Mom asked, *You'd live in sin?*
He hushed.
        At the state fair, he found a pen
of Jacob sheep, four-horned and bearded kin
of goats, and muttered about her god's chagrin
at making caprine sheep and sheepish men.

Mutton

> —*After* Figure with Meat *by Francis Bacon,*
> *The Art Institute of Chicago*

Sheep and goats shuffle down
    a corridor—bumping the walls
and each other, two flocks
    excited or nervous—to meet
their judge, regal and bearded
    like red Pope Innocent X,
but they find Figure—a negative,
    comfortable and probably laughing,

    with a black liquid running
from nose to neck; he might, with ache
    of caprice, take flight on wings
he fashioned from the young
    carcass of one of their kin and crow,
Seekers hunger and you who graze
    can't fill into the loins of every
jostling bovid—instead.

I had such a fun birthday with you—
    always bring me back here, okay?

Mousing

His dead mother's spring traps, well seasoned
with peanut butter daubs, failed their task,

so he pushed a new glue trap behind
the oven and left for a night's work.

After, with a fork, he flicked the trap
onto the floor. Smaller than his thumb,

a mouse lay fixed at its side, right legs
pinned under the skull and ribs. Its shit,

the small, abundant releases, stuck
in like fashion. The pretty gal said

at the hardware store, *These work real good,
though a touch inhumanely.* He pinched

the trap between his finger and thumb
and hoped the mouse still lived till it writhed.

Dammit, he yelped, the trap adhering
his index to the tail, and peeled it

away, straight into a plastic bag.
Outside in the dawn, he heard a squeak

but wouldn't look in the bag. A plea:
*For a favor I'll tell all you want

to know.* He spoke into the plastic,
whispered doubts, then raised it to his ear:

No one can save you. He laid the bag
on the lawn and stomped it with his heel

once, as asked, then twice more to be safe.
The second catch was dead by the time

he got home, the fight fossilized—prints
of clawing, living. A manic heart

bursts as the mind bucks for freedom from
the skull's grip. The third and fourth worked on

breaths and bore no concern for the man
who tossed them into the kitchen trash,

praying for grace and hush unmoving
in the house no one would seize him from.

Figure II

—After Head VI *and* Study for Crouching Nude *by Francis Bacon*

Figure takes flight from the glass box in streaks
    and joins his gathered flock of sheep and goats
below who utter surprise—the longish bleats
    of doubt—content to watch him silently bloat,
mouth off-center for years, but never float.
    Figure creates a creature to take his place
in the box, a bleary, muscled nude, and clothes
    the man in robes and a hat. He offers, *Find
constraint or unleash to eat, or tend, your bovid kind.*

Fungicide Blues

Between a mirror and a window, a woman
    can see herself and nearly all behind her
or just the woods out back where trees wear coats
    of black angels' share fungus. She sips a bourbon,
the last of her father's stash and a reminder
    how space suffused his *uh-huh* replies each morning.
He shaved while she talked and talked, his gaze remaining
    fixed on his own mouth, chin, sideburns, and throat.

Black growths mar white siding on the house
    her father died in, gorging on ethanol
a distillery voids airborne toward each host.
    She treats the stains and in the bathroom places
two mirrors opposite so she gluts that space
    and can't see past herself where the spores fall.

Flight Theory

The big gray dog turns
your building's corner. It barks
then runs for you. You think
to go inside, but a man appears—
the dog retreats to his whistle.

You're driving on your street
when a squirrel skitters out
slower than other squirrels,
its back broken. You brake fast
enough to spill your coffee
and watch the front legs drag
its weight into the grass.

The big gray dog turns
the same corner the next week.
It barks then runs. You wait
for the man. One beat, two,
you make for the door, but
there's the man. He whistles.

You're driving interstate
at eighty miles per hour
when you run over a red stain
sprayed across two lanes.
It's got to be deer, blood
that big—an eighteen-wheeler
on an autumn night. But you're still
surprised how far you must drive
to find the roughed-up pieces
and the head upturned on
the shoulder, as if it never saw
anything but ahead, or even if
you can find time for second thought,
you haven't the space for change.

Backbones

With vertebrae
pinching across

vertebrae,
I see my chiro-

practor, who pushes
and twists the bones

to line, and hear
gases released

into the space
opened between

cervical backbones
snap like firecrackers,

the lymph and fluid
suffusing, back-

filling, and for
the first time all

month, I can feel
nothing back there.

She says, *Apply
ice,* but I won't

remain relieved,
this dull pain, bones

compressed and muscles
knotted and drawn

against my nervous
system, pressure

submerging me
beneath, behind

myself, a constant
longer than I

had known, and yet
I've reveled in

striding across
roots thickened through

the bone-dark skin
of the Earth, slabs

of sidewalk fractured,
upturned, because

a tree has needed
more room to breathe.

Prayer to the Transporter

For a rate, carry our names, one to a body bag, through the spaces that divide somatic and social death. The worst seep and must be double-bagged, constraining their spoil

from the sterile in-between. With a trocar, lord, you lance and empty organs, your varnish washing over the sick, or you incinerate to bone fragments. Lord, someday your work may end,

though not its rituals. You know too well the body's worth—how much it costs to teach a family how much it costs. So many options, so many decisions to make. Conduct us, lord, instead

back to the hospitals and morgues, our home deaths. Stack us high. When our filth can spread, watch us observe the ceremonies—we're all a hearse, a gurney, a legion of ants lifting fifty times

its weight. Good lord, how many would buy the padded box or furnace if social death came first? Only our god could cleanse these debts, let us convey ourselves to earth on cozy plots, to slow-

descend into the dune grass of a favorite river.

The Missouri

I.

He swerves on the bridge and wrecks
in the right lane. Once out,

his sneakers slip on the ice,
just like the semi sliding

his way, its horn blaring.

II.

There's only time for one
foot to the guardrail and over

(the flapping of his coat).
The Missouri shoves along

two hundred feet below.

III.

The smacking, shallow spill
of a flightless bird, hard-rock

grip of the water tamping
his thighs, the neck of his shirt—

plans, fight, the handclap surface
and scream have fled, were carried

past the state park downstream.

IV.

Somewhere a diaphragm,
arrhythmic between the graying

organs and eyes dilated,
treads water, so the four-

lane truss bridge bows
with the weight of ten stopped cars

and the semi (unwrecked
and stalled) in witness to

the grave lacunae of his pupils.

V.

*Naked I shall return
whence I came.* Calves clutch

buttocks, biceps to chest,
neck to shoulder: the womb-

home where mind slides past
confusion, where cell ions

crawlstroke their membranes.

VI.

Geese crowd a boat launch
to rest on the south-trek,

and the river makes east
then south with Mississippi

and much (always) is lost,
abducted to replenish

this basin, his watershed.

VII.

His father and police
man johnboats for eighty days,

their seminary boy
not dead until they find

his body. Fish don't live
much in this passageway

(apathy turned edema),
so it's a trainman that crashes

the bank and scares a flock
from the boy. The geese peck

then flee the dormant grasses
hungry enough to eat

what minerals wash ashore.

Fourth Chamber

Only Not Like This)))

Once in the gray engulfing southern Illinois
highway, we could see gray
(a dozen feet of road then gray) only so I braked
to make time (for what
we called fog until we saw reds flare

within or beyond
what we were (perhaps) starting to understand
as a cloud of carbon
burned to particulate), flipping on my hazards
while we oriented ourselves

by the red (we named fires) dotting the farm-
land west, by the blurting
of fragments about people tending these burns
against the wind (acres
relieved of what remained of a winter's

landscape waste
(that all of it was supposed to happen (only not
like this))) & so on
the last day free for open burning that spring
we grew convinced

of this why we raised & yet I ferried us
(all the same)
through that mile of smoke, fists gripping
the wheel against
whatever grew still on the road.

Consumed

The man across the alley returns home
in his truck each afternoon, his take

overflowing the bed. Some things he casts
into the alley, his garage congested
with sequestered treasures. The discard pile—

a broom, TV, three rotting railroad ties,
particleboard, a ladder-back chair—gathers.

The broken glass—there's always broken glass—
grows, too. Sparrows and robins peck insects
out of the ties. They hop the beams to chip

and pull, possess. In August afternoon,
when birds hide in the trees and flies touch down

to crawl, seeking and seeking, does the wood
possess maggots deposited in the furrows
of the man's refuse? Or still does all this trash—

now just one pile—belong to him? Perhaps
the maggots have the wood in which they eat,

expel, pupate—a childhood home. The truck
is gone and there is violence in the alley.
A robin yanks its take, takes flight, alights

to the glass-strewn concrete to do the breaking
that makes digestion easy. Its stomach can't

be the fly's child's. Birds eat till full then leave.
The man will leave more garbage to feed the pile
flies leave young in. With luck they'll grow enough

to fly away before Tuesday when garbage
men decimate the pile of leavings left

by the skinny man who gathers leavings.
Having leads to filling, full can only
leave, and when no body's satisfied

for good, there's violence in the alley: muggy
heat exudes from the pile because last night

glutted clouds discharged their cleansing waste.
Decay, spurred and untold, all bodies bear
their witness, these bodies all the time beholden.

Nautili

With my pickaxe and gloves I ripped out rotten
    railroad ties all Midwest summer. To base
new bricks I laid, I dug, leveled the ground,
    and tamped fresh chat—pulverized limestone, waste
of miners, and remains of the sea creatures

    that swam above these hills. The new walls held
drainpipes and backfilled earth to stall erosion.
    That fall, after she left for another man,
we slept together once more, and when he called
    the next morning, we lay supine and rigid

in our underwear and stains. She rolled
    to face the drywall and murmured of breakfast
with family. Cephalopods and our beaked mouths,
    the buoyant mollusks striped each time they grew—
more chambers, building more shell until they sank

    to the sea floor, last gases bubbling up
from bones descending. When old walls posed a threat,
    I replaced them, working the ties barehanded,
tamped ground fish-bone-and-fossilized-shell to level.
    Creosote wept by railroad ties rode rainfall

into the ground—these clean stone bulkheads bore
    the earth, my even work coaxing the rain
around a home to a yard where down it coursed
    past sod, dirt, rock, to wash the soiled bones
of what built before—what preserves will poison.

House Centipede

To catch one running out
the corner of your eye,
synchronized orchestration
of leg after hair-thin
leg propelling across
Berber carpet, down
the air vent, is to find
bipedalism means
too few. One six feet up
the wall (resting or sleeping?),
legs like your lashes, the eye
a locomotive core,
means there is time for one
fell death-swat and to revel
in flutter, the falling limbs
and carcass, the indifference
of your perception, arrhythmic
twitter of legs that stick
to the shed hemolymph
staining your shoe, white drywall.

1983

—After Encased – Four Rows *(1983-93) by Jeff Koons*

In the birth year of cell phones, Internet,
the artificial heart (he lived 100
and 12 more days), and me, Koons started making.

While I yawned forth head first from the canal
of my parents' married mistakes, Koons conceived
24 basketballs (of 2 brands and 3

different skin tones) in original packaging,
stacked 4 columns of 6—plus futuristic
building block plastic casing for each ball—

and christened it *Four Rows*. Of such creation
some people say, *Anyone could do that.*
In this case, me: that year suicide bombers

killed 300 in Beirut, 4,000,000
starved in Ethiopia, the IRA
bombed UK Christmas shoppers, and when Koons

was done a decade later, my folks had only
made a basketball team of sons and razed
(like 1/2 a million Americans that year) a marriage,

but I was (sure I was) uniquely angry. It takes
so long to see the constant: encased basketballs,
the minor travesties. How lovely, though,

the singular surprise to tilt one's gaze
and finally see *Four Rows* as 4 rows.

Corn

Corn chips, on the cob,
in a can, the mash bill
of his bourbon he was
expecting, even the feed
of cows turned steak, hamburger
he ate no second thought,
but then his soda, ketchup
(all his condiments),
and the cough syrup, taking
it all down, a cornbread
brain, his bones pureed,
the once-detested creamed
corn simmered, reduced to weight-
bearing—kernels the new
hemoglobin tumbling
through phloem toward pancreas
and broken down, absorbed,
pulsed red, red avarice
the chain to marrow, and if
you look for his grave (not yet
but later)—a stone within
the monocultural field
of stalks stooped with the weight
of massive, pest-resistant
ears—you may find it dead-
center of an earthy
American feedlot.

The Hoarder's Epilogue

A fifteen-passenger van that hasn't moved
replaced his truck. It could be the cold keeps him
indoors—snow weighs on upholstered chairs
someone abandoned for him. A magenta hamper
with a plunger handle sticking out, a yellowed
recycling bin, and the mirror overwinter.
Beneath oaks in the park it's clear, but gingko
seeds in reeking smears remain, their souring
much hastier than acorns'. The Osage oranges
endure—yellow-green tuberculated humps
peeking through snow—but squirrels already
filched their seeds. What good are empty rinds
to *Maclura pomifera,* or are the economies
of salvage, value of color or good taste
more objects in motion? His people bring—
the pile autonomous—and prove what breeds
in absence like wildflowers patching a landfill
hillside. Just yesterday one ditched a leaning
entertainment center, and even animal blood
glue, holding the particleboard compact
like a cyst, may bear the snowpack, and I pitch
this legal pad of petty winter surveillance
without a footprint tracking to my door.

Ribcage

The crumpled metal, nylon and airbag burning
    my clothes and skin, even the glass—some window
worked under my cornea—everything pressing
    in on my body, I scream and let fly what

me can be fled. I've never wanted so much
    to stand, feel pebbled glass roll off my lap
and clatter to asphalt like a thousand chipped
    front teeth. I'm no velocity, a ribcage

driving air in and out the way trees are
    similar mass above ground and below,
the oak behind my mother's house and dogs

    we buried there—first earth, then tree. I root
my nervous system down, and lengthening
    my spine, I grasp for the sun with my sternum.

Preserve

Three bison grazing on valley bunchgrass.
    Cameras poking from windows of cars
idling on the one-way road:

a snow of cottonwood seeds across
    the dale and bison backdropped
by a vacant cherrywood barn.

Downed windows so I could feel
    closer. A pop-up thunderstorm,
buoyant plume of updraft,

that condensed then dropped its crass
    burden of water on the park,
prodding the bovids in

to shelter. Rain driving their smell
    back to earth, rain and dark smearing
most everything from view.

The parade of brake lights crawling
    up the switchbacks and a sign
we pass—*Remain in car.*

Bison have damaged vehicles before.
    How much I have experienced
only inside this glass-and-metal crypt

of a car. The exit betrayed by chain-
    link and barbwire, but the rumble
of a cattle guard made me feel outside.

Attrition

A blue jay chases a crow twice its size,
and all I can remember are the bees
behind my mother's house. We threw

tennis balls at a cavity in the tie wall
they'd staked as home, so they engaged
with us. Some bees fought and died

tangled in my brother's curly hair,
his scalp knotting as I carried him in
after the swarm dispersed. Our mother

taught us to feel guilt, so I practiced
a child's contrition, blaming his swollen
wails on bees. Most bodies get to grow

then wane, instinct enduring, a constant
to provoke each thoughtless action, though
I'll probably disclaim that. Does cross

the road by my mother's house at night—
dim forms at the tree line, a large one
trailed by two fawns learning the path

to her size. I throw on my flashers and wait
their passing. If they balk I frighten them
across or back with a honk. Either's fine

so long as their risk of crossing another
driver is gone, someone who still needs
the yellow sign with a bounding cartoon

buck to perceive their hazard. If action
is outcome, then every instinct is
its consequence, sign or not, but the odds

of two bodies colliding always fluctuate
with population density. Cops turned up
one night on a call about the doe alive

and impaled on my mother's faux wrought-
iron fence. *There's just one thing we can do.*
Because, in part, my mother selected stately,

barb-tipped pickets, we had to dislodge
the whole section so a Public Works crew
could uncouple and dispose of the body.

Fifth Chamber

Uncoupled, the body disposes of this witness, for poison's part and parcel of any preservation. Lift your shoes and jog these rows, my footprints probably track you back to another American feedlot. My sternum felt the outside, Duchamp's comic calculation hahaha I cannot stand to be signified on stained steel when I've been so careful about chronic wasting disease. How's this for a priori: everything's never here, and the population of any choice exceeds two no matter what the brain stem signals, your body never beholden to any one thing except this one. You know how if you have two seeds and you give one sun and water and soil it unfurls a plant but if you give all that then take any of it away, the bunchgrass dies, never regrows, but that other seed remains, no worse for the lack? Stop watching already. In all this flight, you move your body down a road to still, but I've not fled to death. Pray I sought the salty grass that pops roadside these early months after the plow has passed.

About the Author

Clayton Adam Clark lives in St. Louis, his hometown, where he works as a mental health counselor in private practice alongside his spouse, Tina, and their therapy dog, Tank. His debut poetry collection, *A Finitude of Skin*, won the Moon City Poetry Award (Moon City Press, 2018). He earned the MFA in poetry at Ohio State University and a master's in clinical mental health counseling from University of Missouri–St. Louis.

www.ingramcontent.com/pod-product-compliance
Lightning Source LLC
Chambersburg PA
CBHW031429290426
44110CB00011B/583